I NEVER MET A MANDELBREAD

I DIDN'T LIKE!

A Collection of Mandelbread Recipes, History and Trivia

By Michelle Gabriel

Published 2005 by Gabriel Press

ISBN: 0-9643475-2-0

For information about ordering books, visit: www.jfssv.org

When I think of mandelbread (a.k.a. mandelbrodt, mandelbroit, mandl broit, mandelbrat or mandelbrote, to name just a few of the spelling variations), I'm amazed at how a basic recipe of eggs, sugar and flour can take on so many diverse results. By adding oil or butter, almonds or walnuts, raisins, chocolate chips, jam, cinnamon and chocolate, as well as any number of other combinations, you have a variety of mandelbreads that offer its own distinct flavor, taste and memory. And the interesting part...they're all delicious. In fact, I've never found one that didn't make me reach for a second or even a third, because, as the title of this book explains..... I never met a mandelbread I didn't like!

- Michelle Gabriel

Table Of Contents:

Biscotti/Mandelbread Recipes

Passover Mandelbread Recipes

Acknowledgements

I could not have created this collection of mandelbread recipes without the support, encouragement, contribution and assistance from so many people who graciously gave of their time and enthusiasm for this project. Thank you to everyone at Jewish Family Services of Silicon Valley who provided overwhelming support. My gratitude to Andy Pearlman, for her invaluable research skills, Penina Stern and Rachel Engel for their patience in editing this collection, Dimitry Bobroff, for his digital photography, Millie Bobroff for her interest and encouragement and Bonnie Stone for her artistic insights. To my loving husband, Joseph, our children; Ira, Debbie, Aaron, Roberta, Rachel and Alan, and grandchildren; Brittany, Sarah, Brianna, Daniella, Joshua and Jacob, thank you for your undying support of all my crazy projects, and my deepest appreciation to all the wonderful individuals who sent in their "best" mandelbread recipes.

(Parenthesis denotes recipe origin if different from contributor).

Irene Avdienko (Alexandra Bobroff), Jill Becker (Sheila Sacks), Mindy Berkowitz (Evy Mittleman), Fran Blaustein, Irene Bruskin, Carolle Carter, Lillian Cohen (Esther Behr/Nettie Cohen), Nanette Cutler, Joy Danzig, Lucy Delman, Ruth Donenfeld, Hedy Durlester (Barbara Tract), Joanie Eisinger (Arlene Lefkowitz), Bette Emanuel (Ilene Hoffman), Miriam Engel, Harriet Freiman, Lillian Gabriel (Sadie Gabrilowitz), Ruth Gordon (Shelly Schwartz), Susan Green, Eva Grinfas, Gail Hahn, Jenean Hoffman, Judy Bart Kancigor (*Melting Pot Memories*, by Judy Bart Kancigor), Lynn Lertzman (Helen Bessler), Judy Levin, Alisa Zimbalist Levine, Bobi Levine (Lillie Levine, Sid Ruby), Eileen Marks, Elena Falkova-Perelman (Naomi Roman), Sheri Prizant (Jean Prizant), Fagie Rosen (Sophie Van Rosam, Tybil Garshon, Esther Steinberg, Gloria Rosen), Bettina Rosenberg (Ellen Cooper), Harriet Saltzman, Maureen Schneider, Claire Shapiro, Laura Sigura (Sarah Theise), Marilyn Silver (Eva Golden), Diane Simon (Pauline Grant), Rosalie Sogolow (*Memories Of A Russian Kitchen*, by Rosalie Sogolow), Marsha Spector, Sandy Spungen, Penina Stern, Carol Thailer (Tessie Feigin, Lillian Pollak), Shelly Zell (Phyllis Omel).

A special thank you to Robert Hoffman, graphic designer extraordinaire, for his outstanding illustrations, and Lisa Hoffman Harris for her brilliant cover design.

Many, many thanks to you all….Michelle Gabriel

History

I often thought that mandelbread was "invented" or at least "discovered" during the 18th century somewhere in Eastern Europe. However, there is strong evidence that its predecessor was an Italian cookie called biscotti, derived from 'bis' meaning 'twice' and 'cotto' meaning baked or cooked.

According to historians, biscotti was a popular treat in ancient Rome, eventually spreading to other parts of the continent. In fact, over time, many European countries adopted their own version of biscotti including the Eastern European Jewish communities, where recipes took on a variety of ingredients, names and spellings.

Among the Germans, these cookies are known as zwieback; the Dutch call theirs rusks; the French enjoy biscotte and croquets de carcassonne; the Greeks have their biskota; the Spanish have carquinyoles; the Russians have suhariki; and in the Ukraine, it's called kamishbroit or just kamish.

Both biscotti and mandelbread recipes favor the twice-baked route, resulting in a crisp, dry textured cookie with a long shelf life. This similarity between the two makes them identical twins, if not close "kissing" cousins.

Mandel (pronounced Mahn – del) means almond, although the ingredients (in addition to, or in place of almonds) that can be added to these popular cookies are limited only by one's imagination and may include dried fruits, chocolate and jam, as well as different varieties of nuts, seeds and spices.

The twice-baked process that creates the crunchy texture and unique flavor, also makes mandelbread ideal for dipping into tea or coffee. According to Joan Nathan, *Jewish Cooking in America,* "Mandelbrot is literally almond bread and because it was twice baked, it kept well and so became a Sabbath staple for merchants, rabbis and other itinerant Jews who wanted to take a sweet with them during the week."

Today, mandelbread is an easy dessert or snack that can be enjoyed with just about everything. It can be kept at room temperature for several weeks if stored in an airtight bag and while refrigeration is not recommended, it can be frozen and enjoyed right from the freezer.

Either way, in spite of its long shelf life, these cookies are so good, they don't seem to ever hang around for long.

The recipes included in this collection represent a wide variety of favorites from all over the country, including Israel. While many appear similar, the variations (adding nuts, raisins, dried fruit, more eggs, less eggs, once-baked, twice-baked or even thrice-baked) give each recipe its own unique flavor and 'personality'.

I have found that, occasionally, some bakers become slightly possessive about their recipe, certain that theirs is the best of all! Whether or not a specific recipe in this collection meets Webster's definition of "best" (*the most excellent sort; surpassing all others*) is not for me to say, after all, if beauty is in the eye of the beholder, then certainly, "best" when applied to mandelbread, has to be in the taste buds of the eater!

I present the recipes as they were given. The rest is up to you.

Enjoy! – M.G.

Suggestions, Additions, Comments

- While I often refer to mandelbread in its Americanized form, I have used the spelling version of choice as submitted by each participant.

- If a recipe calls for a "handful" (as in raisins and/or nuts), I used a half cup when testing the recipe.

- Some bakers told me they 'mold' the dough into loaves right in the pan or cookie sheet. While I've left that direction as is, when testing, I found it worked better for me if I shaped the dough on a lightly floured board before gently placing on cookie sheets.

- Everyone's oven is different, everyone's take on "golden brown" is different and everyone's concept of "dry" is different. Three people preparing the same recipe will wind up with slightly different versions of the same thing. Some results are more crisp and dry, while others take on a more cake-like texture. The bottom line here is if the ingredients are good, how bad can the end result be?

- All recipes in this book can be made pareve, which means for those keeping kosher, ingredients such as chocolate chips or margarine (look for the kosher/ pareve indication on packaging), can be used when serving meat or dairy.

- Some recipes call for additional baking on the other side of each slice. That is purely optional and according to personal preference.

- When a greased cookie pan was suggested, I used PAM for baking, a no-stick cooking spray with flour.

General Recipes

Two wonderful cooks are credited with this recipe sent in by Bette Emanuel (who remembers my sister, Ilene Hoffman, preparing these mandelbread cookies for her annual Chanukah gatherings) and Shelly Zell (who remembers Phyllis Omel, an icon in the San Jose Temple Emanu-El community, who also shared these cookies on special occasions). Using a cusinart gave a slightly different spin to the recipe, which both Ilene and Phyllis said significantly cut their preparation time in half.

(San Jose, CA)

Phyllis and Ilene's Cusinart Mandelbrot
(Phyllis Omel and Ilene Hoffman)

2 1/2 cups flour
1 tsp. baking powder   * "cuize"
1 stick margarine
1 cup sugar   * "cuize"
1 tsp. vanilla extract
1/2 almond extract   * "cuize"
2 eggs

* (NOTE: "cuize" or pulse: using cusinart until ingredients are blended, approx. 30-40 seconds)

Add nuts, if desired, before removing dough from cuzinart.
Place on floured board and roll into two to three logs depending on size of each log.
Bake at 250 degrees for 20 minutes.
Remove, slice on a diagonal and return to oven for 5 to 10 minutes until golden brown.

Rosalie Sogolow shares this recipe from her book, "Memories Of A Russian Kitchen", published in 1996. This is a wonderful collection of memories and recipes from many of the émigrés who arrived in San Jose from the former Soviet Union. Rosalie's recipe was from a cousin and, as Rosalie wrote in her book... "Cousin Sarah Millman was always such a good cook. If it was one of her recipes, we always knew it had to be good!"
(Saratoga, CA)

Cousin Sarah's Mandel Bread (Almond Slices)
(From "Memories of A Russian Kitchen" by Rosalie Sogolow)

4 cups flour
3 eggs
1 1/2 melted margarine
2 tsp. vanilla extract
1/4 cup Bisquick (Rosalie's addition)

1/4 orange juice
1 tsp. baking powder
slivered almonds
1 cup sugar

Heat oven to 350 degrees.
In a large bowl beat eggs and add sugar, vanilla, orange juice and margarine. Add flour, baking powder, almonds and Bisquick.
Shape into six loaves, about 2 inches to 3 inches wide and 3/4 inches thick.
Place on two ungreased cookie sheets for 20 minutes or until tops of loaves are lightly browned.
Remove, slice on a slight diagonal, place slices on side and return to oven for approximately 20 more minutes until browned.

This recipe, from Miriam Engel, has become the hands down favorite of our friends and family. She says she first tasted it at a friend's house many years ago and has baked it often for many joyous occasions. Whether it's the way she prepares it or the old world flavor that goes in to it, this one has a distinctive taste and crunchiness that is very pleasing.

(Saratoga, CA)

Miriam's Mandelbread
(Miriam Engel)

3 eggs   3 3/4 cup flour
1 1/8 cup of sugar   1 tsp. baking powder
1 cup oil
raisins, nuts (to personal preference)

Mix all ingredients together.
Form dough into three long logs (to fit greased baking pan or cookie sheet).
Bake at 350 degrees for 25 minutes.
Slice on a diagonal and bake an additional 10-12 minutes.

Ruth Gordon doesn't remember where she found this recipe, but she swears she makes it at the drop of a hat. She says it's easy, doesn't take a lot of time and never makes it to the freezer. When her son comes home to New Jersey for a visit, he always takes some back to share with his Los Angeles friends, her daughter takes a batch home with her and, when Ruth's not looking, her husband goes back for seconds and thirds! (Sayreville, N.J.)

Jam, Nut, Raisin and Cherry Mandel Bread
(Ruth Gordon)

3/4 cup sugar
1/2 cup oil
2 eggs
1/4 cup orange juice
Cinnamon/sugar mixture for topping

2 tsp. baking powder
1 tsp. vanilla extract
2 1/2 cups flour

Filling: cup of nuts, cup of raisins and/or cup of cherries,
small jar of grape jam or jam of your choice.
Mix ingredients together.
On a floured board (or on floured wax paper), divide dough into two parts,
roll each part until length of cookie sheet.
Spread filling over dough and roll, jelly roll style and place on ungreased
cookie sheet. Sprinkle top with cinnamon/sugar mixture.
Bake one hour at 350 degrees.
Cool, slice on diagonal. (Resembles strudel.)
OPTION: for extra crispness, return slices to oven for additional baking.

This recipe is one of my own, a recent favorite. Although I am certain it is not original, I have not seen it or heard of it before. For me, it was a combination made in heaven, developed out of a passion for both chocolate and peanut butter and a love of mandelbread. 'Why not?' was my motivation and inspiration.
(Saratoga, CA)

Chocolate Peanut Butter Mandelbread
(Michelle Gabriel)

1 cup vegetable oil
2 eggs
2 tsp. baking powder
1 tsp. vanilla extract
1 Tbsp. unsweetened cocoa
(chocolate chips – optional)

1 1/4 cup of sugar
2 1/2 cups flour
1/4 tsp. salt
3 Tbsps. peanut butter

Mix all ingredients except unsweetened cocoa.

Divide dough into two parts.

Add unsweetened cocoa to one part, mixing well.

Swirl (either with a wooden spoon or knead by hand) the cocoa dough into the plain dough, just enough to give it an interesting marble pattern. Add chocolate chips to chocolate part at this point.

Form into three thin loaves to fit greased cookie sheet.

Bake at 350 degrees for 35-40 minutes.

Remove from oven and allow to cool slightly.

Slice on a diagonal, placing each piece on its side.

Return to oven and bake for 10 to 15 minutes more.

This was my grandmother, Rose Zacker's, standard mandelbread recipe. She didn't read or write English, yet she was able to cook and bake from memory, all the recipes she brought with her as a young bride from Vilna, Russia in 1906. She never twice baked her mandelbread and when I inherited her recipe in the early 1960s, neither did I. Years later, when I first tasted twice baked mandelbread, I realized I liked the extra crunchiness it developed as a result of a few minutes more in the oven. While I have favored the twice baked mandelbread recipes for many years, I still cherish my grandmother's original recipe.

Grandma Rose's Mandelbread
(Rose Zacker)

1 cup sugar   1/2 cup oil
1/2 cup orange juice   3 eggs
3 cups flour plus 1 tsp. baking powder
Add 1/2 raisins and/or chopped walnuts
1 tsp. vanilla or almond extract.

Combine all ingredients.
Turn dough onto floured board and knead for a few minutes.
Dough will be somewhat sticky.
Divide dough into three parts.
Roll each part into long logs and place on lightly greased cookie sheet or baking pan.
Bake at 350 degrees until golden brown.
Slice on a diagonal and serve.
OPTION: can be twice baked.

Judy Bart Kancigor shared this kamish (Ukrainian for mandelbread) recipe for these pretty cookies. They are twisted and require brief baking if formed into very narrow ropes or logs which are then twisted together (this takes some practice). If you make thicker logs, adjust the cooking time accordingly. Thicker logs will take 15 minutes, plus 7 minutes of toasting, while regular size (approximately 2 inches thick) will take 20 minutes plus 5 minutes of toasting on each side depending on one's oven. Either way it's worth the effort.

Sally Cohen's Black and White Kamish Bread
("Melting Pot Memories" by Judy Bart Kancigor)

6 large eggs
2 cups sugar
3/4 cup oil
5 1/2 cups flour
1/4 cup cocoa

5 1/2 tsps. baking powder
2 tsps. almond flavoring
1 tsp. vanilla extract
1/2 cup shredded coconut

Mix all ingredients, except cocoa, in a large bowl.
Divide dough into 2 equal parts and mix cocoa into one part.
Knead both parts well and refrigerate until dough is firm enough to handle (a couple of hours or overnight).
Preheat oven to 350 degrees.
Line cookie sheets with parchment paper or grease.
Roll dough very thin, ideally into a pencil shape.
Gently twist one black roll and one white roll around each other into a spiral, patting gently to hold the spiral together, shaping into long, thin, narrow rolls the length of the cookie sheet.
Bake 10 to 12 minutes. Remove to cooking racks until lukewarm.
Slice on an angle while still warm as they will harden when cool.
Toast slices in hot oven till golden brown.

My childhood friend, Gail Hahn, says this recipe was given to her about 30 years ago while at a play-date with her son David and his classmate's mom. Gail explains that while she and the other mom never kept in touch after they both moved away, the mandelbread recipe, which she uses often, always makes her think about those early years and the play dates with the two little boys.
(Staten Island, N.Y.)

Gail's Favorite Mandelbread
(Gail Hahn)

1 stick butter
1 1/2 cups sugar
3 eggs
1 tsp. vanilla extract
1 tsp. salt
 Cinnamon/sugar mixture

3 cups flour
3 tsps. baking powder
1 cup maraschino cherries
1 cup chocolate chips
1 cup chopped walnuts

Mix all ingredients.
Place dough on floured board and shape into 3 loaves on greased cookie sheets.
Sprinkle with cinnamon/sugar mixture.
Bake at 350 degrees until golden brown, approximately 25 minutes.
Cool slightly before slicing on a diagonal.
OPTION: can be twice baked.

Another friend, Eva Grinfas, lives in Israel and always has something sweet to offer her guests when they arrive at her home. She can make the most elaborate recipe look effortless yet the results are a culinary delight. The following are two of her favorites. This is the one her mother used to make.

(Israel)

Ima's Mandl-Broit
(Eva Grinfas)

4 eggs	1 cup sugar
1 cup oil	3 cups flour
2 tsps. baking powder	A few drops of vanilla extract
Chopped almonds (to preference)	

Mix all ingredients.

Working on a floured board or wax paper, form dough into two long rolls (or loaves) and put in a heated oven under moderate heat (350 degrees).

Bake for 10 to 15 minutes.

Remove from oven and slice on an angle.

Return slices to oven and bake for another 20 minutes or until slightly brown.

Remove, cool and place in tightly closed container.

Eva's second recipe is a modified version she translated from one of her Israeli cookbooks. The 10 egg yolks give it more of a cake like consistency, however, the overall result is quite good...actually, as I reach for another one, the result is down right delicious.
(Israel)

Israeli Mandl-broit
(Eva Grinfas)

4 cups flour	2 Tbsps. baking powder
1 cup almonds finely chopped	1 cup raisins
1 cup sugar	3/4 cup oil
10 egg yolks	4 Tbsps. lemon juice
1 Tbsp. almond extract	pinch of salt

Heat oven to medium (350 degrees).
Put all ingredients in a bowl.
Mix to blend, then knead until the dough becomes even and soft.
If the dough sticks to your fingers, add a bit more flour.
Divide into 4 loaves, shaping to fit baking pan.
Place in pan at least 2 inches apart.
Bake 20-25 minutes.
Remove from oven, cool, then cut into slices.
(The slicing created crumbs when I tested the recipe. Since the crumbs are so tasty, I scooped them up and placed them in a small plastic container, which I froze for future toppings on cobblers and pies.)
Place slices in baking pan and bake for another 20 minutes.
Keep cooled mandlbroit in tight container.

Sheri Prizant's mother-in-law, Jean, always brought these delicious cookies when she came to our house for dinner or other holiday gatherings. They taste like date nut bars and have the ingredients of date nut bars, but they look so much like mandelbread that they just have to be included with all the rest of the mandelbread recipes. Date nut bars or mandelbread, either way, they're delicious.
(San Jose, CA)

Jean's Date Nut Bars

(Jean Prizant)

1 cup butter/margarine	2 cups (8 oz. package) chopped dates
2 cups sugar	3 cups flour
3 eggs	1 tsp. cinnamon
1 tsp. nutmeg	1 cup chopped walnuts
1 tsp. baking soda	2 tsps. water
2 Tbsps. sugar for sprinkling	

Cream butter or margarine, add sugar, add eggs one at a time.
Dissolve baking soda in water and add to mixture.
Add flour, cinnamon, nutmeg. Blend in nuts and dates.
Chill several hours.
Form six, 10 inch by 2 inch long rolls, placing two rolls
each on greased cookie sheet.
Flatten, sprinkle with sugar and bake in a 350 degree oven
for 15 to 18 minutes.
Cut on a diagonal while still hot.

Lynn Lertzman's "Kamish Bread" uses brewed tea as a coating before baking. The recipe was given to her approximately 30 years ago from her friend, Helen Bessler, who got it from her mother-in-law. Once Lynn tasted it, she says she knew she wanted the recipe. "Helen invited me over to not only share her recipe, but to have me make it with her so I'd know how it was done," explains Lynn. "It's been a treat for my family and friends ever since."

(Alameda, CA)

Lynn's Kamish Bread
(Helen Bessler)

Mix together:

3 eggs   1 cup sugar

Add:

3/4 cup oil   2 tsps. baking powder,

1 tsp. vanilla extract   2 1/4 to 2 1/2 cups flour

1 cup chopped walnuts.

Cinnamon/sugar mixture for topping

Mix well and refrigerate at least one hour.

Flour two cookie sheets and form dough into 4 long rolls.

Bake at 375 degrees for approximately 1/2 hour until golden brown.

Brush with brewed tea and sprinkle with cinnamon/sugar mixture.

Slice diagonally, place on cookie sheet and bake at 325 degrees for additional 15 minutes to toast.

OPTION: use sliced almonds and 1/2 teaspoon vanilla plus 1/2 tsp. almond extract in place of 1 tsp. vanilla extract and chopped walnuts.

Alisa Zimbalist Levine makes this recipe every Friday night. "While most people call this mandelbrot, my family calls it Kamishbroit, or just Kamish. The recipe's simple, delicious and frankly," she adds, "without it, it just wouldn't be Shabbat." Alisa's mother got this recipe from a cousin and baked it every week, using pecans in one loaf, keeping the second loaf plain. Both were baked for 40 minutes. Later, Alisa created the chocolate chip version and decided it tasted better a little less well done. Her daughter, who has taken over as chief Kamish baker of the family, loves craisins, which has become her new tradition. Alisa's husband says the recipe tastes better with each new generation! (Needham, MA).

Kamishbroit (Shabbat) Recipe
(Alisa Zimbalist Levine)

3 eggs	1 cup sugar
3 cups flour	2 tsps. baking powder
3/4 cup vegetable oil	
Raisins or craisins and chocolate chips	
Cinnamon/sugar mixture	

Mix all ingredients in order listed (except last part), using a wooden spoon. (You may need to use your hands as the dough will be thick). Divide dough in half.

Add 1 cup raisins or craisins to half the dough and 1 cup non-dairy semi sweet chocolate chips to the other half. Mix well.

On a greased cookie sheet, shape dough into two loaves, approximately 2 inches wide, to fit length of cookie sheet.

Sprinkle cinnamon/sugar mixture on top of loaf containing fruit.

Bake in preheated 350 degree oven for 15 minutes. Remove, slice and return to oven for additional five minutes.

NOTE: While this version is pareve, adding other variations, such as, M&Ms and peanut butter chips (Alisa's husband and son's favorites), makes the recipe dairy.

Irene Bruskin grew up eating Grandma Gert's Mandelbrat, which she believes originally came from her great-grandmother. "I loved watching my grandmother bake, and mandelbrat was what she often made. I once asked her the reason for making the well in the middle and, of course, there was no reason except that was how her mother did it. I usually don't bother with the well, but I included it in the recipe for the sake of nostalgia." Irene's maternal great-grandparents came from Russia, although her grandmother was born in Manhattan and raised in the Bronx.
(Ridgewood, NY)

Grandma Gert's Mandelbrat
(Irene Bruskin)

3 eggs
slightly less than one cup of oil
1 tsp. lemon juice
1/2 tsp. salt
1/2 cup raisins
1 – 2 Tbsp. sugar/cinnamon mixture

1 1/2 tsp. baking powder
1 cup sugar
3 cups flour
1/2 cup nuts

Preheat oven to 350 degrees.
Combine dry ingredients in a large bowl.
Make a well in the center and add eggs and oil.
Mix well. Dough will have a firm consistency.
Fold in nuts and raisins.
Form into loaves.
Brush lightly with water.
Sprinkle with cinnamon/sugar mixture.
Bake for 30 minutes. Slice loaves on an angle and turn slices on sides.
Return to oven and bake an additional 10 minutes or until
desired crispness is reached.

Marsha Spector describes this as a very simple mandelbrodt recipe that she's been making for at least 35 years. "I think I got it from my grandmother, Sonia Cohen or her sister, Kate Talcott," Marsha explains. Since she has given the recipe to anyone who asks for it, she says it's possible that it may have worked its way around the world by now, or at least throughout the California Jewish community! Marsha's cookies have traveled well to many Hollywood Bowl concerts where her friends eagerly anticipate intermission, a cup of coffee and her mandelbrodt! (Toluca Lake, CA)

Marsha's Mandelbrodt
(Marsha Spector)

4 eggs	3 cups sifted flour
1 1/4 cup sugar	1 1/2 tsps. baking powder
1 tsp. vanilla extract	2 Tbsps. orange juice

1 cup blanched almonds or walnuts coarsely chopped.

Beat eggs well. Add everything but the nuts.
Mix with a spoon until blended. Stir in nuts.
Mixture will be soft. Divide dough into 4 equal parts.
Sprinkle flour on a board and on hands.
Working with one part of the dough at a time, quickly shape dough into a long roll, about 8 inches long and 1 1/2 inches in diameter.
Place roll crosswise, evenly spaced on a 15x10x1 inch jelly roll pan. Bake at 375 degrees, about 1/2 hour or until golden brown.
Remove from oven. Trim off brown edges from dough and cut while warm into 1/2 inch slices.
Carefully remove slices to another jelly roll pan, arranging close together cut side down.
Toast at 325 degrees, 15 to 20 minutes.
Turn slices over when underside is light brown.
(Watch to prevent burning.)

This was my mother-in-law, Sadie Gabrilowitz's, recipe, shared by her daughter in New York and her two daughters-in-law in California. She made them often when she came out from the east coast to visit her two sons and their families over the years. My sister-in-law, Lillian Gabriel, sent a copy of the original recipe to me in our mother-in-law's clear, perfect handwriting.
(Brooklyn, N.Y.)

Sadie's Mandel-Brote
(Sadie Gabrilowitz)

4 eggs
1 cup vegetable oil
1 tsp. almond extract
Juice from one lemon and rind
4 cups flour
1/2 tsp. baking soda
Cinnamon/sugar mixture

1 cup sugar
1 tsp. vanilla extract

3 tsp. baking powder
1 cup nuts (and/or raisins)

Mix all liquid ingredients, then gradually add dry ingredients
with nuts and/or raisins.
(Chill dough if not ready to bake)
Form dough into three long rolls, size of baking pan.
Brush tops with a little oil, sprinkle with cinnamon/sugar mixture.
Bake at 325 degrees.
When lightly golden, slice into diagonal pieces and return to
oven until browned.

While Nanette Cutler enjoys making several different kinds of mandebrot all year round, she describes this one as a "real winner." That sentiment was unanimously echoed by a group of women with whom I "tested" this recipe. Part macaroon, part cookie, part cake, this one received high praise.
(Encino, CA)

Almond-Apricot Mandelbrot
(Nanette Cutler)

3/4 cups flour   1 1/2 cups sugar
1/2 cup (1 stick) chilled unsalted butter or margarine, cut into pieces
1/2 tsps. baking powder   1 tsp. salt
tsp. ground ginger   2 large eggs
1/2 oz. white chocolate chips
2/3 cups toasted almonds (whole)
1/4 cup plus 1 Tbsp. apricot flavored brandy (or peach brandy instead)
tsps. almond extract
6-oz. package dried apricots, diced.

Combine first 6 ingredients in food processor to create a fine meal.
Add white chocolate chips and process until finely chopped.
Add toasted almonds and chop coarsely.
In a separate bowl, beat eggs, brandy and extract.
Add flour mixture and apricots, stirring until moist dough forms.
Drop spoonfuls of dough onto greased and floured pans, forming long strips.
Shape each strip into 2-inch wide logs. Refrigerate until dough is firm
(approximately 30 minutes).
Bake at 350 degrees until golden (approximately 30 minutes).
Cool completely, reduce heat to 300 degrees.
Cut each log crosswise into 3/4 inch-wide slices. Return slices to cookie sheet and
bake an additional 10 minutes. Cool and store in airtight container at room
temperature.

Fran Blaustein's Aunt Marion made mandlebread for everyone in the Pepper Family. She was famous for her mandlebread. "Whenever my aunt visited our home she would bring mandlebread in tin cans, which I sometimes hid from my family," Fran explains. "When we moved to California, I asked my aunt for the recipe. I have tried to duplicate the recipe and have made it at least 500 times. My family and friends think my mandlebread is very good. I think of my aunt when I make her recipe and hope I am doing her proud. My family thinks I'm crazy for giving up this recipe because they think I could be the next Mrs. Fields!"

Aunt Marion's Mandlebread
(Fran Blaustein)

1 cup vegetable oil
2 eggs
2 tsps. baking powder
juice from 1/2 large fresh lemon
large handful of chopped walnuts
handful of raisins

1 cup of sugar
2 1/2 cups flour
1/4 tsp. salt
2 tsps. vanilla extract

Mix oil and sugar with wooden spoon in medium to large bowl until well blended, add eggs and mix well.
Add all the flour at once and sprinkle with baking powder and salt, mixing well. Add vanilla extract, then nuts and raisins, continuing to mix well.
Cover, refrigerate for a couple of hours or overnight.
When ready, form dough into 2 long thin loaves and place on a greased cookie sheet or Reynolds release liner silver foil.
Bake for an hour at 325 to 350 degrees depending on oven, until lightly browned.
Remove from oven and slice on angle.
Place slices on their sides baking again at 300 degrees for 20 minutes.
Remove from oven and cool.
Mandlebread may be kept in the freezer in boxes or tins.

This is another one of those recipes that fall under the category of...why not? After experimenting with the chocolate peanut butter mandelbread recipe, it was a matter of time before someone, in this case, my daughter, suggested trying a mint chocolate chip variation. Both recipes come out very dry (so watch the rebaking time), but we loved them anyway, crumbs and all.
(Saratoga, CA)

Mint Chocolate Chip Mandelbread
(Michelle Gabriel)

1 cup vegetable oil
2 eggs
2 tsps. baking powder
2 tsps. mint extract
1/2 cup chocolate chips

1 1/2 cups of sugar
2 1/2 cups flour
1/4 tsps. salt
4 Tbsps. unsweetened cocoa

Mix all ingredients together.
Form into three thin loaves, place on greased cookie sheet.
Bake at 350 degrees for approximately 35 to 40 minutes (depending on oven).
Remove from oven, cool slightly, then slice on the diagonal.
Place each slice on its side on cookie sheet and return to oven
for an additional 10 to 15 minutes (depending on how crisp
you prefer).

This recipe was given to Ruth Gordon by her good friend, Shelly Schwartz, who unfortunately passed away several years ago. The two women met as young newlyweds in a Brooklyn apartment house, "kvelled" (proudly rejoiced) together over their children and remained close friends even after they moved from Brooklyn to bigger and better places in New Jersey and Long Island. Ruth says that whenever their two families got together, they always knew there would be chocolate chip mandelbread for dessert. Now whenever she makes this, it is a tribute to the memory of her friend.

(Sayreville, N.J.)

Shelly's Chocolate Chip Mandel Bread
(Shelly Schwartz)

2 cups flour   4 large eggs
1 cup sugar   1/4 cup oil
1 tsp. baking powder
1 1/2 cups chocolate chips
Cinnamon/sugar mixture

Preheat oven to 350 degrees.
Grease 2 large cookie sheets.
Mix all ingredients together.
Using wet hands, form into 4 loaves.
Sprinkle cinnamon/sugar mixture on top.
Bake for 25 minutes, depending on oven.
Remove from oven and slice on an angle, placing
each slice on its side on cookie sheet.
Return to oven for 5-10 additional minutes.

Penina Stern's mother made a type of mandelbrot that she called strudel.
Penina says she may have learned to make it at her mother's knee,
because her Grandmother owned a bakery in a small shtetl (village) in
White Russia (now part of Poland). According to Penina, the bakery
was considered the hub of 'important' events in the town during the late
eighteen hundreds.
(Los Gatos, CA)

Penina's Mother's Mandelbread
(Penina Stern)

3/4 cup oil	1 cup sugar
2 eggs	2 cups flour
2 tsps. baking powder	2 tsps. vanilla extract
pinch salt	juice of 1/2 lemon and rind
1/2 cup nuts	1/2 cup raisins

Mix all ingredients together.
With floured hands, form 2 long loaves about 3 inches wide
and bake on greased cookie sheets at 350 degrees for 30-40 minutes or
until lightly browned.
While warm, cut into 1/2 inch slices and return to 200 degree oven for 1 to
2 hours until crisp.

Every time Carol Thailer makes her grandmother's mandelbread, she says she's flooded with happy memories. "It was not an easy task extracting the recipe's ingredients and proportions from her, since she never used a written recipe." What Carol and her mother finally resorted to was to have the grandmother stop at every step so they could measure and record the quantity of each item being added. After assembling the cursory recipe, they tried it out and finalized it only after they were satisfied that it tasted, smelled and looked like "grandma's mandelbread recipe."

(San Jose, CA)

Grandma's Chocolate Chip Mandelbread
(Grandma: Tessie Feigin and Mother: Lillian Pollak)

3 eggs	1 cup sugar
1 cup oil (Crisco)	2 tsps. vanilla extract
3 cups flour	2 tsps. baking powder
3/4 cup chopped walnuts	1 cup mini-chocolate chips
Mixture of cinnamon/sugar	

Beat eggs. Mix together eggs with oil, sugar and vanilla.
Add flour and baking powder, mix well.
Add walnuts and chocolate chips.
Place bowl in freezer for 15 to 20 minutes. Then shape dough into 6 small cylindrical rolls with floured hands.
Place on a large greased cookie sheet.
Bake at 350 degrees for 35 minutes or until light brown.
Slice each roll while warm.
Place slices on side and sprinkle each side with cinnamon/sugar mixture.
Bake an additional 5 – 6 minutes.

Diane Simon recalls spending many happy afternoons with her sister baking with their mother, Pauline Grant, whom they both agree was a wonderful baker. This recipe was first printed in a cookbook in her sister's Temple in Connecticut over 40 years ago.
(San Jose, CA)

Diane Simon's Mondel Bread
(Origin unknown)

1 cup sugar	1/2 cup oil
3 eggs	1 tsp. vanilla extract
1/2 tsp. salt	3 1/2 cups flour
3 tsps. baking powder	1/2 nuts (optional)

3 squares baking chocolate (melted)
1/2 cup sugar for topping

Mix sugar, eggs and oil.
Mix flour, baking powder and salt into egg mixture.
Add vanilla extract.
Divide dough into thirds, reserving some dough.
Flour board or wax paper and flatten dough on to it, one third at a time.
Mix reserved dough with melted chocolate and remaining 1/2 cup sugar.
Place some of the chocolate dough in middle of each flattened dough, adding nuts if desired.
Roll dough up, jelly roll style.
Sprinkle tops of each roll with sugar.
Bake in 375 degree oven for approximately 25 minutes until lightly browned on top. Dough will crack slightly on top.

Judy Levin, a wonderful cook on her own, shares this recipe from her Aunt Beulah in Chicago. "It was passed down to my mother from my aunt, and everyone in our family decided that this was their favorite mandel brot recipe," explains Judy.
(Livermore, CA)

Aunt Beulah's Mandel Brot
(Judy Levin)

1 stick butter plus 1 stick margarine
1 cup sugar   3 eggs
1 tsp. vanilla extract
3 cups flour   1/4 tsp. baking soda
1/2 tsp. baking powder   1/2 tsp. salt
3/4 cup chopped toasted almonds
Mixture of cinnamon/sugar

Place 2 inch by 6 to 8 inch logs of dough on parchment lined baking sheets.
Sprinkle logs with cinnamon/sugar mixture.
Leave several inches between logs.
Bake at 350 degrees for approximately 20 minutes or until golden brown.
Cool 10 minutes on wire racks and cut on the diagonal into 1 inch bars.
Place in 325 degree oven and toast on both sides until dry.

Eileen Marks has been making this recipe for over 20 years, ever since she was given the recipe from a sisterhood member from Congregation Etz Chaim in Marietta, GA. After moving away from Georgia, Eileen started to bake the cookies, but discovered that she had lost the original recipe. Fortunately she had passed the recipe on to her mother and sister, who came through at the last moment and saved the day, and the cookies!

(San Jose, CA)

Eileen's Mandelbread
(Eileen Marks)

2 1/2 cups flour   1/2 tsp. salt
2 tsps. baking powder   3 eggs
6 Tbsp. oil   1 cup sugar
1 tsp. vanilla or almond extract
1 cup or more craisins or chocolate chips or both

Preheat oven to 350 degrees. Flour a cookie sheet.
Mix all wet ingredients. Add salt and baking powder.
Gradually incorporate flour into the batter.
Fold in craisins and/or chips. Dough should be on the wet side,
but not gooey. It should hold its form when placed on cookie sheet to bake.
With wet hands, form an almond shaped loaf on the cookie sheet using half
of the batter. Do the same for the rest of the batter, leaving room between
the two loaves for dough to expand and rise. (Eileen suggests using two
different cookie sheets and staggering the time they enter the oven).
Bake for 40 minutes.
When each loaf is done, remove from oven, slice and place slices on cut
side.
Raise oven temperature to 450 degrees and return slices to oven, keeping an
eye on mandelbread to prevent from burning.

Laura Sigura says this recipe was given to her mother, Berta Wesler, by her mother's best friend, Sarah Theise, at least 30 years ago. Laura's mother has baked it ever since. "It must be a great recipe," says Laura, "because Sarah and my mother are still best friends!" (Sunnyvale, CA)

Laura's Mother's Friend's Mandelbrot
(Berta Wesler/Sarah Theise)

1 cup sugar	1 cup oil
3 eggs	2 tsps. baking powder
1/2 tsp. salt	6 cups flour
3/4 cup orange juice	

(all ingredients at room temperature)

Have ready: 2 pound jar strawberry preserves, cinnamon
and sugar mixture, raisins or currants and 8 oz. chopped walnuts.

Mix eggs and sugar. Add oil and juice, then dry ingredients.
Divide dough into 4 parts.
Roll out the first part, spreading a little oil on top.
Spread jam over dough, add cinnamon and sugar, raisins and nuts.
Roll up tightly but slowly.
Repeat with other three parts. Spread aluminum foil on cookie sheet.
Bake at 375 degrees for 40 minutes (check at 30 minutes). Slice on
diagonal. (Can be returned for additional baking if desired.)

Jill Becker shares this story. Her daughter Beth's mother-in-law, Sheila Sacks, had planned on making this family favorite at home in Capetown, South Africa, before leaving to visit her children in Birmingham, England. When the cookies didn't come out just right, she packed the ingredients and, immediately upon her arrival at the children's home, went into the kitchen and proceeded to make the promised mandelbread. Once the dough was in the oven, she and her husband had to leave with the family, leaving Jill behind to watch over the mandelbread still baking. Having never made mandelbread before, Jill says she was very nervous. Following Sheila's carefully written instructions on slicing and returning the sliced mandelbread to the oven, Jill is pleased to report that not only did she survive the challenge, but the mandelbread was a big hit around the family table that evening. (San Jose, CA)

Sheila's Italian Mandelbrot
(Sheila Sacks)

1 cup egg whites (about 6)	1 cup sugar
1 1/3 cup sifted flour	1 tsp. vanilla extract
1/2 cup blanched almonds (can be toasted if desired)	

Preheat oven to 325 degrees.
Beat egg whites until they are stiff but not dry.
Gradually beat in sugar and then the vanilla extract.
Fold in the sifted flour and then the nuts.
Line base of a loaf pan with parchment paper.
Spray or grease sides. (I used four mini loaf pans)
Pour mixture into loaf pans.
Bake approximately 35 minutes or until lightly browned.
Turn oven off and leave in oven for 20 minutes to cool.
Remove from pan when cooled and slice into very thin slices.
Place slices back in pan and return to cool oven (approximately 250 degrees) to toast until lightly golden.
(Can substitute chocolate chips for nuts.)

Claire Shapiro's Grandma Gold, came to the lower east side of New York from Russia at the end of the 19th century as a newlywed. Her neighbors were mostly Jewish, Irish and Italian. While her Irish neighbor taught her English, her Italian neighbor taught her how to bake. Grandma Gold's version of the Italian Biscotti recipe soon became the family's traditional Mondelbread recipe.

Grandma Gold's Mondel Bread
(origin unknown)

2 eggs
1/2 cup oil
1/3 cup sugar
1 tsp. vanilla extract

1/2 cup chopped walnuts
1/2 cup raisins
1 1/2 cups flour
1 heaping tsp. baking powder

Mix all ingredients together.
Form into three loaves and place on a greased cookie sheet.
Bake at 350 degrees until brown (approximately 20 minutes).
Remove from oven and slice into strips.
Return slices to cookie sheet and toast each side under the broiler for a few minutes.
Watch carefully to avoid burning.

Hedy Durlester sent this in, crediting Barbara Tract, a good friend who sadly passed away at a young age. Hedy often made these mandelbread cookies which she brought along on long beach weekends shared with another family. She later found out that, unbeknownst to her, two of the weekend guests (including her son) would often hide the cookies from each other, causing a shortage of these delicacies for the rest of the crowd. "I kept baking and bringing more and more cookies each time we went up," she says, "but it never seemed to be enough!"
(Santa Rosa, CA)

Barbara's Mandel Brodt
(Barbara Tract)

2 eggs
1/2 cup vegetable oil (Canola)
2 1/2 cups flour
1 cup walnuts (or any other kind)
orange rind (optional)
Cinnamon/sugar mixture

1/4 cup sugar
1 tsp. vanilla extract
1 tsp. baking powder

Mix all ingredients. Roll on floured board.
Place on parchment covered cookie sheet and bake at 350 degrees
for 30 minutes.
Cut on a diagonal and sprinkle with cinnamon/sugar mixture.
Return to oven for additional 10 minutes.
Turn oven off and leave in for another 5 minutes.

NOTE: A heavy duty mixer such as KitchenAid is recommended.
If dough seems wet to the touch, add a little more flour, up to 1/2
cup only if needed. Hedy does not make this recipe when it's
raining, because she says it seems to absorb too much moisture
from the air.

Bobi Levine's mother, Sid Ruby, learned to bake mandelbread the old fashioned way from her mother, Bobi's grandmother, using two flavors of dough rolled around each other. These cookies were great to dunk into a cup of hot chocolate or coffee, as they were well toasted. Bobi says her mother kept bags of mandelbread in the freezer and always brought a bag or two with her whenever she visited anyone.
(San Jose, CA)

Sid's Mandelbread
(Sid Ruby)

4 eggs	1 cup sugar
1 tsp. vanilla extract	pinch of salt
3 1/2 cups flour	1/2 cup oil
4 tsps. baking powder	3 Tbsps. cocoa
1 cup chopped nuts (walnuts or almonds)	

Beat eggs, add sugar, salt and vanilla extract.

Add 1/2 amount of flour (1 3/4 cups) unsifted.

Add oil, then other half of flour with baking powder.

Mix the nuts in by hand.

In a separate bowl, add cocoa and mix with 1/4 of the batter.

Divide white dough into long loaves about 2 inches thick.

Roll chocolate dough into long snakes.

Place the chocolate dough on top of the white dough that was first patted into a sheet 1/2 inch thick.

Place loaves on a greased cookie sheet and bake at 325 degrees for approximately 20 minutes.

Cookies are done when tops begin to crack.

Remove from pan and while warm, slice diagonally, toast on each side, 275 degrees for approximately 15-20 minutes.

Bobi Levine shares another Mondel Broit version, this one from her mother-in-law, Lillie Levine. Bobi says Lillie, who was famous for her mondel broit cookies, always had a #3 coffee can full of cookies ready to send home with any visitor who stopped by to visit. "She meticulously packed them into a coffee can, layer by layer, placing them carefully so that they wouldn't break into pieces. Her recipe was in her head, she didn't measure ingredients and no one knew what she might add to embellish the flavor if she ran out of one of the basic ingredients. In order to capture this recipe, I sat and measured everything that she placed in the bowl. She loved to cook and bake and was forever sending home to us some delectable goodies that she had prepared."
(San Jose, CA)

Lillie's Mondel Broit
(Lillie Levine)

3 cups sugar   6 cups flour (1 cup at a time)
1 1/2 cups shortening (1/2 vegetable oil -1/2 peanut oil -1/2 Crisco oil)
6 large eggs   3 tsps. almond extract
3 tsps. vanilla extract   3 tsps. baking powder
1/4 tsp. baking soda   1 tsp. salt
2 Tbsps. sour cream (or cottage cheese)
3 Tbsps. orange juice (liquor or other fruit juice)
Mixture of cinnamon/sugar

Place above ingredients in a mixer and mix well.
Add 1 pkg. chocolate chips (1 1/2 cups) and 1 1/2 cups chopped
almonds or walnuts.
Chill dough overnight in bowl. Sprinkle top lightly with flour and cover
with wax paper.
Divide dough into quarters with spatula, roll and divide each quarter into
thirds. (Form into loaves) and roll onto 1/2 sugar and 1/2 cinnamon mixture
sprinkled on breadboard.
Place 3 rolls (loaves) on oiled cookie sheet and bake for 15 minutes
in 375 degree oven until lightly brown. (Repeat with remaining loaves).
Slice hot and toast on a cookie sheet for 15 minutes in 350 oven. Watch
closely and turn as needed.
Place hot cookies in coffee cans with tight lids.

Lucy Delman learned to make this recipe from her mother, although she admits that when she first started baking it, hers always seemed to crumble as she sliced it. After experimenting with several variations as well as other recipes, she settled on this one. She makes it often and has helped many other women learn to bake it as well. "The beauty of mandelbread," she says, "is that it is relatively simple to put together and its crunchy texture is very satisfying to the palate, especially with a dessert of stewed fruit or ice cream and of course, with a cup of coffee or tea."

(San Jose, CA)

Lucy's Mandelbread
(Lucy Delman)

3 large eggs
1 cup sliced almonds or chopped walnuts
1 cup sugar
1/3 cup vegetable oil
1 tsp. almond or vanilla extract
2 1/2 to 2 3/4 cups flour
1 tsp. salt
1 tsp. baking powder
Finely grated rind of lemon or 1/2 orange rind (optional)
Sugar/cinnamon mixture (optional)

Preheat oven to 350 degrees (325 for dark pans).
Beat eggs at high speed until light and lemony in color.
Slowly beat in sugar, oil, extract, rind and nuts.
Mix in flour, salt and baking powder, blending on low speed
(or by hand using a wooden spoon).
With lightly floured hands, form dough into three long rolls
(about 2 inches wide and 3/4 inches high).
Bake on greased cookie sheets until lightly browned (approximately 20 to
25 minutes).
While still warm, cut diagonally into 1/2 inch slices, sprinkle with sugar/
cinnamon topping and return to oven for additional 10 minutes.

Marilyn Silver got this recipe from her mother, Eva Golden, who had gotten it from her mother, Dora Lipsitz. Marilyn is not sure of the origin, but guesses it was from a relative in Warsaw, Poland where the family had lived. Now Marilyn says that the next generation, her daughters Karen and Deborah, are successfully continuing the family tradition.

(Laguna Woods, CA)

Dora's Mandelbroit
(Eva Golden/Dora Lipsitz)

In a large bowl, sift:
3 cups of flour
1 cup sugar
2 tsps. baking powder
Make a well in the center of dough, add 3 large eggs
1 cup oil
2 tsps. vanilla extract and 1 tsp. almond extract.
Mixture of cinnamon/sugar for topping

Place dough on an ungreased cookie sheet.
Divide dough into 2 long loaves to fit cookie sheet (each loaf
approximately 2 inches wide).
Sprinkle top with 1 tsp. cinnamon and 3/4 cup sugar, saving some for later.
Preheat oven to 350 degrees.
Bake for 25 minutes.
Remove from oven (turn oven down but not off).
Cool, then cut into diagonal slices. Place slices, side down, on cookie
sheet, sprinkling with additional cinnamon and sugar mixture, and return
to oven for 10 minutes. Turn oven off, but leave mandelbroit in until oven
is cold (this makes the slices crisp).
NOTE: Almond slices or mini chocolate chips may be added.

Harriet Saltzman remembers her grandmother, who was from Latvia, baking mondel bread, a long time family favorite. "My mother then continued the tradition, making these often because they are great to dunk in tea, and my father was a tea drinker." Harriet says she has made these for all the wonderful family occasions, as well as for friends who had mitzvahs to celebrate. The reason she included several options for the recipe is because of the many dietary restrictions she encountered. "I usually make one roll with chips, one with nuts, one with raisins and nuts and one plain for those who can not tolerate the other ingredients." (San Jose, CA)

Harriet's Mondel Bread
(Harriet Saltzman)

3/4 cup oil	1 Tbsp. almond extract
1 cup sugar	2 beaten eggs
1 heaping tsp. baking powder	2 1/4 cups flour

Optional ingredients: nuts, raisins, chocolate chips

Mix oil and sugar.
Add eggs and mix well.
Add almond extract and mix.
Sift and add flour and baking powder.
At this time, add any of the above options.
Grease cookie sheets.
Spoon into long rolls onto cookie sheets and, with wet hands, mold smoothly.
Bake at 350 degrees, plus or minus, for 25 to 30 minutes.
Cut while warm into diagonal slices, separating slices slightly. Place under broiler for a few minutes to dry, watching carefully to avoid burning.

Millie Bobroff, my running (then jogging and now walking partner) for over 20 years, asked her sister-in-law, Irene Avdienko, for the family suhariki (Russian for mandelbread) recipe, which was a favorite during the holidays. "My mother, Alexandra Bobroff, used to make these mostly at Christmas time," Irene explains. "She brought the recipe from China where she spent her childhood and young married years. When she grew old, she stopped making the suhariki because, she claimed, they never came out right. The insides weren't crisp enough, she told us." Now when Irene makes suhariki, she cuts off a little piece to check the inside after baking them for thirty minutes. If the dough looks moist, she puts the cookie sheet back into the oven for another ten minutes. (Valley Springs, CA)

Irene's Mother's Suhariki
(Alexandra Bobroff)

Cream together:
3 eggs
1 cup sugar
Add 2 cubes (sticks) of melted butter
1 tsp. cinnamon
Dash of salt
1/2 cup (or more) chopped walnuts
1 tsp. baking powder
6 cups of flour

Mix all ingredients well.
Separate dough into four rolls.
Place onto a greased baking sheet.
Form rolls into long logs and flatten to approximately
1 1/2 to 2 inches wide.
Preheat oven to 350 degrees. Bake for 30 minutes.
If suhariki are not done, bake additional 10 minutes.
Slice (on a diagonal) while dough is hot.
Place in oven again with heat off, for half an hour to overnight for
guaranteed crispness.

Elena Falkova-Perelman is originally from Charkov, Ukraine. Naomi Roman, a volunteer who helped Elena and her husband, Rafail, study English for the past 10 years, also became a good friend. Elena says that Naomi gave her this recipe and since then, she is very happy to have the mandelbread with her "coffee and New York Times daily."
(San Jose, CA)

Elena's Friend's Mandelbread
(Naomi Roman)

Cream together:
1/4 pound + 2 Tbsps of butter.
1 cup of sugar
Add 3 eggs
1/4 tsp. baking soda
Mix all ingredients by hand
Add 3 cups of sifted flour plus 1 tsp. baking powder
to creamed mixture
Add 1 tsp. vanilla extract plus a handful of chopped walnuts.

Divide into six parts.
With floured hands, form into 6 long flat loaves and place three each on 2
greased baking sheets.
Bake at 350 degrees for approximately 40 – 50 minutes until golden brown.
Remove and slice into 1/2 to 3/4 inch slices.
Toast under broiler until lightly browned.
(This will happen quickly, Elena points out, "so watch
carefully so as not to burn!")

Fagie Rosen sent in the following three recipes. The first recipe was one from her mother, Sophie Van Rosam, who often made them for the family in Toronto, Canada. After Fagie moved to California, her mother brought them each time she visited and then, ultimately after moving here as well, she continued to make them for all family celebrations. (San Jose, CA)

Fagie's Mother's Mandel Broit
(Sophie Van Rosam)

3 eggs	1/4 tsp. salt
1 cup sugar	3 1/2 cups all-purpose flour
1 cup oil	2 tsps. baking powder
1 tsp. vanilla extract	1/2 cups chopped almonds
1/2 tsp. almond extract	cinnamon/sugar mixture

Beat eggs and sugar until creamy. Add oil, vanilla and almond extract, salt and flour (sifted with baking powder).

Mix in chopped almonds. Flour board and form into 4 or 5 rolls about 12 inches long.

Bake on oiled cookie pans in 350 degree oven for approximately 30 minutes until light brown.

Remove from oven and slice into 1/2 inch slices.

Place slices on cookie sheet and sprinkle with cinnamon/sugar mixture. Return to oven until lightly browned. Turn slices over and sprinkle the other side with cinnamon/sugar mixture and brown again.

Fagie Rosen's second recipe is from her bubbe, Tybil Garshon and aunt, Esther Steinberg, also from Toronto, Canada. Fagie says her bubbe used walnuts in her recipe because it was most likely easily accessible at the time, however, when her aunt started making the mandelbread, she switched to chocolate chips because she was allergic to nuts. (San Jose, CA)

Fagie's Bubbe's Mandel Bread
(Tybil Garshon)

3 cups flour   1/2 cup almonds (or chocolate chips)
3 tsps. baking powder   3 eggs
1/2 cup sugar   1 cup oil

Mix eggs, sugar, oil, baking powder into flour.
Knead by hand on a floured board, forming a smooth dough.
Separate dough into 4 rolls (or loaves). Place on cookie sheet
and bake at 350 degrees for 25 minutes until golden brown.
Remove from oven, lower oven temperature to 150 degrees.
Slice loaves and return to oven and brown for one hour.

Fagie's sister-in-law, Gloria Rosen, lives in Louisiana and has been baking her grandmother's mandelbread recipe for all the special family occasions, including Fagie's visits. While Fagie admits to never having baked any of these recipes, now that she's retired, she's looking forward to trying each one and carrying on the family tradition.
(San Jose, CA)

Fagie's Sister-in-law's Mandel Brot
(Gloria Rosen)

3 cups flour	1 1/2 tsp. baking powder
1 cup oil	1 cup sugar
4 eggs	1 tsp. vanilla extract
1 1/2 cup chopped pecans	
Cinnamon/sugar mixture	

Mix dough together and refrigerate overnight.
Grease baking sheets.
Form long logs (loaves) approximately 1 inch wide.
Bake at 350 degrees for 22 minutes.
Cool and slice on a diagonal.
Sprinkle with cinnamon/sugar mixture.
Return to oven to brown.

The book wouldn't be complete without at least one recipe bowing to the low-carb craze that has been sweeping the country. This Whole Wheat Mandelbread recipe is tasty, healthy and easy to prepare. What could be better than that?

(Saratoga, CA)

Low-Carb Whole Wheat Mandelbread
(Michelle Gabriel)

1 cup sugar
1 tsp. grated lemon peel
2 1/2 cups whole wheat flour
1/2 tsp. baking soda
1/2 tsp. salt
1 cup of chopped walnuts
(Optional - half cup of raisins)
Cinnamon/sugar mixture for topping

1/4 cup butter or margarine
1 tsp. vanilla extract
1 egg (or 2 egg whites)
1 tsp. baking powder
1/2 cup orange juice

Beat 1 cup sugar and margarine until light and fluffy.
Add vanilla extract, lemon peel and egg, mix well.
Add flour, baking powder, baking soda, salt and orange juice.
On a floured board, divide dough and shape into three long loaves.
Place on lightly greased cookie sheet and sprinkle with cinnamon/sugar mixture.
Preheat oven to 350 degrees.
Bake for approximately 30 to 40 minutes.
Remove, cool slightly, and slice diagonally.
Place slices on cookie sheet and bake for additional
10 minutes on each side.

Biscotti Recipes

Here's where it gets a little tricky. Technically the following are biscotti recipes (slightly drier), however, they have either been adopted as is, or "tweaked" to resemble more of a mandelbread version. Regardless of how they are defined, they are delicious. This one for example, a recipe I've had for many years, uses cranberries which makes it ideal for the fall, especially around Thanksgiving. Actually it works very well during winter, spring and summer too!
(Saratoga, CA)

Cranberry Almond (Biscotti) Mandelbread
(origin unknown)

Combine in medium mixing bowl:

2 1/2 cups flour	1 cup sugar
1 tsp. baking powder	1/2 tsp. baking soda
1 tsp. cinnamon	1/2 tsp. nutmeg

Wisk together:

2 eggs	2 egg whites

1 Tbsp. almond extract
Add to dry ingredients, mix thoroughly.
Add 6 oz. (fresh or frozen cranberries)
3/4 cups sliced almonds

(NOTE: I found it helpful to knead dough by hand to help incorporate cranberries and shape logs.)
On a floured surface, divide batter in half, forming into two (or three) long logs to fit cookie sheet.
Bake at 350 degrees for 30 minutes or until firm.
Reduce oven to 300 degrees, cut into 1/2 slices on the diagonal, return to cookie sheet and bake an additional 20 minutes.
Cool and store loosely in a covered container.
Option: blueberries can be used in place of cranberries.

Penina Stern shares this recipe and story from Lillian Cohen. "Lillian was at a social function talking to Nettie Cohen about her favorite subjects: cooking and baking. Nettie gave her the recipe for her famous (biscotti) mandelbrot. Lillian doesn't remember trying it because she had a favorite recipe that she received from another friend. After some years, Lillian became very friendly with a caterer whose name is Esther Behr. She tasted Esther's mandelbrot and says she went berserk! It was delicious, she decided. Esther gave Lillian the recipe, which turned out to be the same one she had had all those years from Nettie."
(Los Gatos, CA)

Lillian's Mandelbrot (Biscotti)
(Esther Behr/Nettie Cohen)

Cream together:

1 stick butter	1 cup sugar
Add 4 large eggs, well beaten	2 cups flour
1/2 tsp. baking powder	1/4 tsp. salt.
2 tsp. vanilla	1 to 2 cups of sliced pecans

Mix all ingredients well.
Divide batter and place onto 2 greased loaf pans.
Bake at 350 degrees for 35 min.
Cool till lukewarm.
Slice diagonally - 1/2 inch thick.
Put slices onto cookie sheet and toast one side for
approximately 10-13 minutes, repeat on other side.

Joy Danzig has been baking mandelbrot for a long time, using a recipe handed down by her mother, who got it from her mother, whose father had a large bakery in Austria more than a century ago. Having tried different recipes over the years, she recently began making a variation on "Meshuganah Mandelbrot" from Marlene Sorosky's "Fast and Festive Meals for the Jewish Holidays". Influenced by the biscotti "craze" (the anise flavoring), Marlene says this is a blended recipe with what might seem to be a lot of steps, but, as she points out, "it is easy and moves along very quickly."

(Santa Rosa, CA)

Joy's Mandelbrot with a Biscotti Twist
(Joy Danzig)

In a food processor, blend:
1/2 cup canola oil   1/4 cup sugar
1/4 Splenda
(Scrape sides with a spatula)
Add 1 large egg   1 1/2 tsps. vanilla extract
1/2 tsp. anise flavoring   1/2 tsp. orange flavoring
Mix well, set aside.
In a medium bowl, whisk together:
1 1/2 cups flour   1/4 tsp. salt
1 tsp. baking powder   2 tsps. finely grated orange zest
1/2 cup nuts (toasted slivered or sliced almonds)
1/2 cup chocolate chips (mini or regular).

Gradually add flour mixture to the oil/sugar, pulsing four or five times, until well integrated.
Remove batter and place in bowl that contained the flour mixture, kneading slightly to blend in any stray flour if needed.
Add nuts and chocolate chips.
Cover with plastic wrap and chill in refrigerator for at least an hour or overnight.
Preheat oven to 350 degrees.
Spray or grease a cookie sheet (insulated or doubled sheet recommended).
Divide dough in half and, with oiled hands, make two long, narrow loaves, leaving plenty of space in between.
Bake for 20-25 minutes, until lightly browned.
Remove, reduce oven heat to 325 degrees. Let loaves set, approximately 5 minutes, slice diagonally, about 3/4 inches wide or to preference.
Bake an additional 10 to 20 minutes.
Remove from oven, and cool (they will harden as they cool).

Susan Green got this recipe from her step-sister, Mary Peters. "Mary gave this as gifts every year for the holidays and it's my favorite recipe," Susan explains. "Because of the use of butter, the results are a little more moist than regular biscotti."
(Woodside, CA)

Susan's Almond Biscotti
(Mary Peters)

1/3 cup butter/margarine
2/3 cup sugar
2 eggs
1 cup sliced almonds

1 tsp. vanilla extract
2 cups flour
2 tsps. baking powder

Mix butter, sugar, eggs and vanilla together.
Sift flour and baking powder.
Add flour mixture to butter mixture.
Mix in almonds.
Shape dough into a log and bake at 375 degrees for 25 minutes.
Cool for one hour.
Cut log into 1/2 inch slices and place face down on a cookie sheet.
Bake at 325 degrees for 8 minutes.
Turn slices over and bake another 8 minutes.
Cool and serve.

When our wonderful Jenean Hoffman married my nephew Robert, our family not only inherited one terrific gal, but one delicious recipe as well. The recipe belonged to her grandfather and Jenean was allowed to watch him bake these Italian cookies until she was nine, then she was allowed to make the entire recipe herself, under grandpa's close supervision, of course. Jenean's grandfather was a carpenter who brought his passion for precision to everything he did, including weighing the dough to make sure it was exactly even when separating it into two parts. Jenean carries on his legacy today, happily making them for the family gatherings, still, of course, under his loving and watchful supervision!
(Roseville, CA)

Baglietto Biscotti
(Grandpa "Tampa" Baglietto)

3 cups flour	3 eggs, slightly beaten
1 1/2 cups sugar	1 cube butter, melted
3 tsps. baking powder	1 tsp. vanilla extract
1 cup chopped walnuts	2 Tbsps. whiskey

Preheat oven to 350 degrees.

Grease 2 large cookie sheets.

Sift flour, sugar and baking powder together.

Mix in nuts.

In a separate bowl, mix wet ingredients.

Combine dry and wet ingredients. Mixture should be fairly dry.

Mix with hands.

Divide dough into 4 equal parts.

Roll each part into a long strip, the length of cookie sheet.

Two strips to each cookie sheet. Flatten each strip to about 1/2 inch thickness.

Bake for 22 minutes. Remove from oven.

Increase oven temperature to 380 degrees. Remove from cookie sheets and cut into 3/4 inch pieces. Place pieces on their edge on cookie sheet and bake for 8 more minutes.

Cool completely on baking racks and store in airtight container.

This is a recipe I couldn't resist, a combination biscotti-mandelbread with a Polyniasian attitude. A true melting pot of culinary ingredients. (Saratoga, CA)

Chocolate Dipped Coconut Macadamia(Biscotti)Mandelbread
(Michelle Gabriel)

3 eggs	3/4 cup oil
1 cup sugar	1/2 cup coconut flakes
1 tsp. vanilla	3 1/2 cups flour
1 Tbsp. baking powder	1/4 tsp. salt

1/2 cup pineapple juice (or orange juice)
1 cup chopped Macadamia nuts (I used chocolate covered)
Semi sweet chocolate for dipping (I used Ghirardelli)

Mix together eggs and oil.

Add sugar, vanilla extract and pineapple juice.

Slowly add flour, baking powder, salt, coconut flakes and nuts.

Place dough on floured board to knead until smooth.

Return to bowl and refrigerate for at least one hour.

On a floured board, divide dough in two three long thin logs and place on greased cookie sheet.

Preheat oven to 350 degree and bake for approximately 25 minutes or until golden brown.

Remove from oven and place logs on a cutting board. Slice diagonally and return slices to cookie sheet, cut side up. Bake an additional 10 to 15 minutes until crisp.

To melt chocolate: Break baking bar of chocolate into small sections into double boiler over 1-inch simmering water.

Stir constantly until melted and smooth (do not overheat).

Carolle Carter sent in this recipe. It's a new twist on a centuries old (biscotti/mandelbread)recipe, starting with a commercial cake mix as the foundation and your imagination to complete the rest. When testing this, I found I needed a little more liquid to create a workable dough, so I added 1/4 cup of orange juice, which worked out just fine. Also, I divided the dough into two long loaves instead of one, as suggested in Carolle's original recipe. The results: A very lemony, cake-like mandelbread that is quite tasty.

(Los Altos, CA)

Carolle's Citrus Biscotti (Mandelbread)
(Carolle Carter)

1 package lemon cake mix
1 Tbsp. vegetable oil
1/4 cup of orange juice,
2 Tbsps. grated lemon peel
1 Tbsp. grated lime and orange peel
Lemon Glaze (see below)

Heat oven to 350 degrees. Mix all ingredients except glaze in a large bowl with a spoon until dough forms.
Shape dough into 2 long loaves, 1/2 inch thick, on a large non-greased cookie sheet.
Bake 20 to 25 minutes, until golden brown. Cool on cookie sheet for 15 minutes.
Cut dough crosswise into 1/2 slices. Arrange slices, cut side up, on cookie sheet. Bake 7 to 8 minutes or until bottoms are light golden brown.
Cool 5 minutes, then turn slices over, bake again for 7 to 8 minutes.
Cool completely, about 15 minutes. Drizzle with lemon glaze and let stand about 4 hours until glaze sets.

Lemon Glaze: 1/4 cup Rich and Creamy Lemon Ready to Spread Frosting. 2 to 4 tsp. lemon juice. Mix together until thin enough to drizzle.
OPTION: German Chocolate cake mix (add mini chocolate chips and dip into melted chocolate), or a white or yellow cake mix (add small pieces of dried apricot and dried cranberries.

Judy Levin shares another one of her favorite recipes, Chocolate-Pistachio Biscotti (Mandelbread), which she's made several times. "They taste yummy and, because of the green nuts, look really great," she says. This recipe makes a huge amount so Judy recommends making half the recipe if you don't want a lot of wonderfully tempting cookies hanging around!

(Livermore, CA)

Judy's Chocolate-Pistachio Biscotti (Mandelbread)
(Judy Levin)

1 pound butter (margarine)	2 cups sugar
4 eggs	4 cups flour

1 cup cocoa
2 cups chopped pistachios (may be toasted)
3 cups semisweet chocolate chips
1 cup sugar and 1 cup finely chopped pistachios for coating

Preheat oven to 350 degrees. Line cookie sheet with waxed paper or parchment.
In medium bowl, cream butter (margarine) and sugar.
Add eggs one at a time, blending well.
Add flour and cocoa powder.
Mix until ingredients are well incorporated.
Add chopped pistachios and chocolate chips.
Divide dough in half and roughly shape each half into a log.
Mix together sugar and finely chopped pistachios and spread mixture on a work surface.
Roll the dough in mixture to form a firm log (approximately 2 inches wide).
Place on cookie sheet, bake until firm, approximately 30 minutes. Remove from oven and cool. Reduce oven temperature to 300 degrees. Cut each log on the diagonal into 1/2 inch-wide pieces.
Place on flat side of baking sheet and bake until firm in center and lightly toasted on top (approximately 10 minutes).

Passover Recipes

Passover

Passover is the eight-day observance commemorating the freedom and exodus of the Israelites (Jewish slaves) from Egypt during the reign of the Pharaoh Ramses II.

A time of family gatherings and lavish meals called seders, the story of Passover is retold through the reading of the Haggadah. With its special foods, songs, and customs, the seder is the focal point of the Passover celebration. Passover begins on the 15th day of the Jewish month of Nissan.

Taking place the first two nights of this eight-day holiday, the seder is the most important event in the Passover celebration. Gathering family and friends together, the seder is steeped in long held traditions and customs.

Leading up to the first night of Passover, the home is cleaned and cleared of all yeast foods, called hametz (generally foods used throughout the year other than at Passover). Only foods that are "Kosher for Passover" are allowed. No leavened (containing yeast) foods, grains, or corn syrup are to be eaten. In their place, matzah and foods containing matzah are eaten. This is to commemorate the Israelites who fled quickly into the desert with no time for their breads to rise and were forced to bake the dough into hard crackers in the desert sun.

When it comes to mandelbread recipes, Passover is a whole other ballgame. While many recipes convert nicely from hametz to kosher for Passover (by substituting matzah baking products for flour, baking powder or baking soda), it is often just easier to start fresh with a recipe specifically designed for the holiday. The good news, though, is that once made, Passover goodies can be eaten all year round.

PASSOVER CONVERSION SUGGESTIONS:

<ins>Instead of</ins>	<ins>Use</ins>
Bread crumbs	Matzah Meal
Graham cracker pie shell	Passover cookie/cake crumbs
Flour	Matzah Meal/CakeFlour/Potato Flour
Stuffing	Matzah Farfel

Ruth Donenfeld's recipe came from her mother who liked to have mandelbread with tea after dinner. It has remained a favorite of Ruth's as well as her sisters who remember having it every year for Passover. Originally the recipe called for peanut oil, but when the oil made Ruth ill, her mother made it either with butter or pareve oleo (margarine). Ruth prefers it with oleo, and says her sister likes it with butter, but half the amount because that makes it drier and more like biscotti. Adding the fruit keeps it moist.

(Orlando, FL)

Fruit and Nut Mandel Bread for Passover
(Ruth Donenfeld)

2 cups sugar
1/2 cup butter/pareve margarine
6 large eggs
2 1/4 cups matzo cake meal
1/2 cup chopped, dried fruit
 Mixture of cinnamon/sugar

1/2 tsp. salt
1 cup chopped nuts
1/2 cup raisins
3/4 cup potato starch

Cream sugar and butter or margarine.
Add eggs one at a time, beat well after each addition.
Sift cake meal, potato starch and salt together.
Add cake meal mixture to egg mixture.
Beat well, batter will be thick.
Fold in nuts and dried fruits.
Shape into two-inch wide logs and place on a greased cookie sheet.
Sprinkle sugar/cinnamon mixture, on top of logs.
Bake at 350 degrees for 45 minutes.
Slice while still warm, place on racks to cool.
OPTION: place slices back on cookie sheets and brown in hot
oven for 5 – 8 minutes or until golden brown.

For many young families migrating west from the East Coast in the late 1950s and early 1960s, banding together became 'de rigueur' if they wanted to establish a surrogate Jewish family so far from home. Temple and synagogue sisterhoods throughout the communities became meeting places where young couples and families grew into long time friends and extended families. Holidays were shared along with traditions and favorite recipes. Over time, many of these shared recipes were "mimeographed" and made into handouts to help others prepare new and old holiday favorites. This is one of those recipes from a Temple Emanu-El Sisterhood pamphlet, circa late 1960s.

(San Jose, CA)

Pesach Banana Nut Mandelbrot
(Origin unknown)

2 ripe bananas	3 eggs
1 tsp. cinnamon	3/4 cup oil
3/4 cup sugar	1/2 tsp. salt
3/4 cup cake meal	3/4 cup chopped nuts
2 Tbs. potato starch	1/4 cup matzah meal

Mash bananas. Beat eggs and sugar together and add to bananas.
Beat in oil.

In another bowl, mix dry ingredients together then add to bananas,
eggs, sugar and oil. Refrigerate at least one hour.

Shape dough into 3 long rolls (or loaves) and place on lightly oiled cookie
sheet. Bake at 350 degrees for 30 minutes or until lightly browned. Cool
slightly.

Slice rolls and place cut side up on cookie sheet.

Return to oven until lightly browned and crisp.

OPTION: use one tablespoon lemon or orange rind in place of cinnamon.

Bettina Rosenberg says her mother's Passover mandelbrot is "good enough to eat all year round". Her mother, Ellen Cooper, made this recipe every year at Passover for as long as Bettina can remember. Now Bettina hosts her own seders and her mother brings the mandelbrot with her when she comes to California from New York. They have experimented by substituting chopped dried fruit instead of chocolate chips and nuts, which tastes good too, Bettina says, but can burn easily. "In our family, we have a tradition associating special foods with particular holidays, so we only make this mandelbrot on Passover, just like we only make latkes on Hanukkah and hamentaschen on Purim. It's a nice way of teaching children about holidays and encouraging them to look forward to each occasion."

(San Jose, CA)

Bettina's Mother's Passover Mandelbrot
(Ellen Cooper)

1 1/4 cups sugar
6 eggs
3/4 cup potato starch
1 cup chopped nuts
Mixture of cinnamon/sugar

1/2 lb. margarine
2 3/4 cups cake meal
6 oz. chocolate bits
1/2 cup raisins

Preheat oven to 350 degrees.
Cream sugar and margarine together.
Add eggs, one at a time.
Fold in cake meal and potato starch.
Add chocolate bits, nuts and raisins.
Form two loaves and sprinkle with cinnamon/sugar mixture.
Bake one hour or until brown.
While warm, cut into thin slices on the diagonal.
Lay slices on its side on a cookie sheet, sprinkle with cinnamon/sugar
mixture, toast in oven for a few minutes.

Mindy Berkowitz says she and her friend Evy Mittleman, make no other baked dessert for Passover but this recipe. It has been handed down so many times they don't recall from where it originated. "We just know that our families gobble this up and mine love it year round," Mindy explains. "It's not only easy to make, it's a great way to use leftover cake meal!"
(San Jose, CA)

Evy's Passover Mandel Bread
(origin unknown)

3 eggs, lightly beaten

1 cup peanut/vegetable oil, (not olive oil)

pinch of salt

1 cup chopped nuts - almonds or walnuts

(Mindy uses different kinds, even peanut butter)

1 – 2 Tbsp. jelly of choice

Cinnamon/sugar mixture for topping

1 cup sugar

1 cup cake meal

3/4 - 1 tsp. cinnamon

Mix all ingredients well and allow to set in the bowl for about 20 minutes
before spreading it into a baking dish.

Use a 9 x 13 inch baking dish lightly greased with oil.

Bake at 350 degrees for 40 minutes.

Can be cut when still slightly warm or completely cooled.

Top with cinnamon and sugar.

NOTE: For the jelly, Evy uses strawberry, Mindy sometimes uses cherry.

My cousin, Harriet Freiman, makes this often for Passover. She says neither her mother nor mother-in-law made mandelbread as far as she can remember and she isn't sure where she got this one from, but she knows she's had it for a long time. She uses Splenda in place of sugar during most of the year, but points out that since Splenda is not kosher for Passover she reverts back to sugar for Passover baking.
(Cleveland, OH)

Harriet's Passover Mandel Bread
(Origin unknown)

1 cup sugar
1 cup oil
1 1/2 cups cake meal
1 tsp. vanilla extract
3/4 chopped nuts - pecans or walnuts

3 eggs
3/4 cup potato starch
1/2 cinnamon
1/2 tsp. almond extract

1/4 cup cocoa (omit if you want vanilla mandelbread or hold out some dough for the cocoa and combine for a marble-like mandelbread).

Combine ingredients in order and mix.
Shape into 3 loaves (about 1 to 2 inches in diameter) on wax paper.
Wrap up loaves and place in refrigerator until ready to cook.
Can sit over night.
Remove from wax paper and bake on lightly greased cookie sheet at 350 degrees for 30 minutes.
Cool slightly, cut into small slices on an angle, and return to oven for approximately 10 minutes. This makes a crisp mandelbread.

Irene Bruskin offers another one of her favorites. She likes this Passover recipe the best because she says it doesn't taste like the usual Passover baked goods. She got it from her step-father's mother who was originally from Russia. Irene has been making this recipe for at least 20 years and says it is always a hit, "even with people who aren't Jewish." This recipe can be either dairy or pareve depending on whether you use butter or pareve margarine.
(Ridgewood, NY)

Irene's Passover Chocolate Chip Mandelbrat
(Irene Bruskin)

2 cups sugar	6 eggs
1/2 pound unsalted butter or pareve margarine	
2 3/4 cups Passover cake meal	
3/4 cup potato starch	1/2 tsp. salt
6 ozs. chocolate chips	1 cup chopped nuts
Mixture of cinnamon/sugar	

Preheat oven to 350 degrees.

Cream margarine (or butter) with sugar.

Add eggs, one at a time.

Sift meal, salt and starch. Fold into eggs.

Mix in chocolate and nuts.

Dough will be a little soft and difficult to work with.

Wet hands and form into loaves. Place on greased cookie sheets.

Brush with milk or water and sprinkle with cinnamon/sugar mixture.

Bake for 45 minutes.

Slice loaves, turn slices on sides and return to oven for 10 minutes.

OPTION: turn slices again and bake an additional 10 minutes.

Joanie Eisinger remembers the early '70s when her mother decided to try Arlene Lefkowitz's mandelbread recipe from Temple Isaiah's cookbook. "I'm so glad she did," explains Joanie, who says she was wowed as a child because she couldn't believe she was giving up hametz while eating this scrumptious chocolate chip cookie. "I began baking in my early teens and Arlene's mandelbroit quickly became part of our yearly Passover seder dessert spread." Joanie has baked the loaves for several decades and now serves them at her family seders.
(Berkeley Heights, N.J.)

Joanie's Passover Chocolate Mandel Bread
(from Arlene Lefkowitz, Temple Isaiah Cookbook, circa 1970, Stony Brook, L.I., N.Y.)

1 1/2 lbs. (8 sticks) butter or margarine (Joanie prefers butter)
2 3/4 cups matzah cake meal
3/4 cup potato starch
6 eggs
2 3-ozs. bars bittersweet chocolate, cut into small pieces (may substitute 6 oz. chocolate chips)
2 cups sugar
1/2 tsp. salt
1 cup chopped nuts (walnuts work well)
Mixture of cinnamon/sugar

Cream sugar and butter or margarine.
Add eggs, one at a time, beating after each addition.
Sift cake meal, salt and starch together. Fold into egg mixture.
Add chocolate and nuts. Mix well. Form into loaves 2 inches wide.
Sprinkle with cinnamon/sugar mixture.
Bake on greased cookie sheet (or parchment paper) in 350 degree oven for 45 minutes.
Slice while warm into 1/2 inch pieces.

Maureen Schneider sent this one which she explains came via New Jersey from Sylvia Fried who is known throughout the community as a fabulous cook. Everyone always asks Maureen to bring these very delicious cookies to seders or even dinners during Passover. She says that they are so good, people have been known to make them all year long. "My nephew is now married to Sylvia's niece, who is one of my best friend's daughters and we joke that it's because he tasted the mandelbrot at my seders over the years. You've heard the expression, the way to a man's heart is through his stomach...here's the proof!"
(Saratoga, CA)

Maureen's Passover Chocolate Nut Mandelbrot
(Maureen Schneider)

2 cups sugar

6 eggs

6 ozs. mini chocolate chips

1 cup chopped walnuts

Mixture of cinnamon/sugar

1/2 lb. margarine

2 3/4 cups matzah cake meal

Cream sugar and margarine.

Add eggs one at a time, beating after each.

Sift dry ingredients. Fold into egg mixture.

Add chips and nuts and mix well.

Form batter into 2 or 3 loaves, 2 inches wide, on a
greased cookie sheet.

Sprinkle with cinnamon/sugar mixture.

Bake at 350 degrees for 35 to 45 minutes (check after 35 minutes).

Slice while warm.

Return slices to oven to dry or crisp to your liking (usually 10 minutes on
each side.) Check to see that they don't get overdone.

Nanette Cutler loves this one for Passover but admits she makes it all year round. The recipe comes from the cookbook, "From Noodles to Strudels" a project of the Beverly Hills Chapter of Hadassah. Nanette has changed the recipe to include dipping or rolling each slice in cinnamon/sugar and baking the mandelbrot an extra 10 minutes on each side for additional crispness.
(Encino, CA)

Nanette's Passover Mandelbrot
(From "Noodles to Strudels" a project of the Beverly Hills Chapter of Hadassah)

6 large eggs
1 1/2 cup oil
1 cup matzah meal
1 Tbsp. potato flour
Mixture of cinnamon/sugar

1 1/2 cups sugar
1 cup chopped almonds
1 cup cake meal

Mix all ingredients in order listed and refrigerate for 2 hours
until dough thickens.
On a cookie sheet, place two, 6 x 14 inch heavy aluminum foil sheets.
Fold up 1 inch on all sides, pinching corners together to form
2 baking tins. (Mixture is not thick enough to stand alone).
Fill each tin with 1/2 the batter.
Bake at 350 degrees for 30 minutes or until cake tester comes
out clean.
Remove mandelbrot from foil.
Cut into 1/2 inch slices and return to oven for additional 10 minutes
on each side.
OPTION: Before returning to oven, dip mandelbrot slices in
cinnamon/sugar mixture.

Penina Stern's Passover mandelbrot recipe came from a very old cookbook she had when she and her family lived in New Jersey many years ago. Penina says the recipe caught her attention because of the use of cloves among the ingredients.
(Los Gatos, CA)

Penina Stern's Passover Mandelbrot
(origin unknown)

1/4 lb. butter or substitute
4 whole eggs
2 cups chopped walnuts
1 tsp. cloves
Powdered sugar

3/4 cup sugar
2 cups matzah meal
1 tsp. vanilla extract

Combine ingredients and form into two long loaves.
Place in greased oblong pan and bake in 350 degree oven.
Moisten hands with water to smooth top surface.
Bake until brown at sides.
Cool and cover with powdered sugar.
Cut in slices.

Sandy Spungen doesn't remember where or when she got this recipe but sayes she knows it's a very old one. "My (recipe) index card has seen better days," she explains, "but I haven't had the heart to rewrite it on a nice white card. I brought this recipe with me from Indiana and my children and grandchildren tell me they love this recipe."
(San Jose, CA)

Sandy's Passover Mandel Bread
(origin unknown)

3 eggs

1/2 cup oil

1 orange (grated rind and juice)

1/3 cup potato starch

1 cup chopped nuts (optional)

Cinnamon/sugar mixture for topping

3/4 cup sugar

1/2 tsp. cinnamon

1/4 cup cake flour

Beat eggs, add sugar and oil, orange rind and juice.

Add dry ingredients.

Place in freezer for approximately 1 hour or more.

Divide dough into 3 loaves on a Pam sprayed cookie sheet.

Bake at 350 degrees for 35-40 minutes.

Cut each loaf on the diagonal while hot, turn each section on its side and sprinkle with cinnamon/sugar mixture.

Bake for 15 minutes, turn on the other side and bake for another 15 minutes. Mandel bread will be crispy

Mandelbread Trivia

* Benoit Mandelbrot is the name of an IBM scientist and Professor of Mathematics who is credited as the "key Chaotician of our times" (the Geometry of Chaos). While neither he nor his discovery have anything whatsoever to do with mandelbread recipes, he is, according to his daughter-in-law, Rebecca, "often given mandelbrot when he travels and lectures around the world."

* Benoit Mandelbrot, now 80 years old, traces his family name back to his grandfather who lived around 1850 in Vilna, Poland.

* Historians confirm that almonds were known to ancient middle eastern cooks and were incorporated into many recipes. They were popular delicacies in ancient Roman times and the popularity of almond biscuits (twice baked hard breads) eventually spread with the Romans to other parts of the continent.

* Because of the dryness of mandelbread (as well as biscotti and other twice-baked goodies), this particular food item traveled well in ancient times and was thereby popular among soldiers, merchants and other traveling members of the respective societies during that period.